Original title:
The Healing Heart

Copyright © 2024 Swan Charm
All rights reserved.

Author: Liisi Lendorav
ISBN HARDBACK: 978-9916-79-273-5
ISBN PAPERBACK: 978-9916-79-274-2
ISBN EBOOK: 978-9916-79-275-9

Rays of Celestial Hope

In the morning light, grace descends,
Whispers of peace, where love transcends.
Hearts awaken to gentle grace,
Guided by faith, we find our place.

Stars above, a faithful guide,
In every prayer, our hearts abide.
The promise of joy, though trials will be,
United in spirit, we shall be free.

The Covenant of Rebirth

From ashes we rise, renewed and whole,
Embracing the light that mends the soul.
With each new dawn, a chance to begin,
In the depths of love, we find our kin.

The waters of mercy cleanse our hearts,
In divine embrace, the old departs.
A journey of faith, we walk hand in hand,
Together we stand, a righteous band.

Treasures of the Spirit

Deep in the heart, where wisdom gleams,
Life's true treasures are birthed in dreams.
In moments of silence, the spirit speaks,
In gratitude's glow, the soul truly seeks.

To share in the grace, a radiant gift,
In loving communion, our spirits lift.
The wealth of compassion, pure and bright,
Guides us through shadows, into the light.

Mosaic of Mercy

Every shard of life, a story untold,
In the tapestry woven, the heart turns bold.
With threads of kindness, we weave and mend,
Each piece reflects love, our truest friend.

Together we gather, the broken and healed,
In the garden of mercy, our fates are sealed.
As colors unite beneath heavens' dome,
In unity, diversity finds its home.

Whispers in the Wilderness

In shadows deep, where silence dwells,
The Spirit speaks, as anguish swells.
Among the trees, a call divine,
In gentle rustles, love does shine.

The river flows with sacred grace,
Each ripple tells of His embrace.
The mountains bow, their peaks aglow,
To worship Him, our hearts can know.

Through desert winds, His voice can be,
A whisper soft, like sweet decree.
With every step, the path unfolds,
A promise kept, in truth, it holds.

In night's embrace, the stars proclaim,
Each twinkle bears a holy name.
The moonlit glow a guiding light,
In darkest hours, He'll hold us tight.

So venture forth, in faith we tread,
With every breath, the Spirit led.
In wilderness, our souls are found,
In whispered prayer, we stand profound.

The Search for Grace

Upon the dawn, our hearts awake,
A quest for grace, for love's sweet sake.
Through trials faced, our spirits rise,
In humble hearts, true beauty lies.

The path is long, with winding turns,
In every heart, the passion burns.
With open hands, we seek the light,
In every shadow, hope ignites.

Through tears we learn, through love we grow,
In sorrow's depth, His kindness flow.
A melody, both soft and clear,
In every loss, His presence near.

The hands that heal, the words of peace,
In every breath, our doubts release.
To find the grace in everyday,
In simple acts, we carve the way.

And so we rise, with faith renewed,
Our hearts adorned with gratitude.
For in this life, the search we bear,
Will lead us home, to love laid bare.

The Garden of Renewal

In the stillness of the morn,
New blooms awaken, softly born.
Whispers of hope in every petal,
Life's fragile dance, a joyful medal.

Hands of faith reach for the sky,
Tending dreams, as seasons fly.
Every tear, a seedling sown,
In God's embrace, we find our home.

Roots entwined in sacred soil,
Where love's essence begins to toil.
In shadows deep, light gently glows,
Nurtured hearts, a sweet repose.

From thorny paths, new blooms arise,
A testament under heaven's skies.
Every breath a sacred prayer,
In the garden, we learn to share.

Fleeting moments, forever stay,
In nature's hand, we find our way.
Renewal springs from every end,
In this garden, soul's roots mend.

Threads of Grace

In the tapestry of life, we weave,
Threads of grace, when we believe.
Each color shines, a story told,
Love unites, as hearts unfold.

With every stitch, a prayer is spun,
Binding souls, two become one.
Hope and courage intertwined,
In faith's embrace, our strength we find.

Through trials faced, the fabric frays,
Yet mercy mends the broken ways.
A touch of kindness, a gentle hand,
In the silence, we understand.

We gather strength from shared despair,
In the hollow dark, God's light is there.
With open hearts, we choose to see,
The beauty deep in unity.

So let us cherish every thread,
In this grand design that God has spread.
Together we rise, in love's embrace,
In every moment, we find grace.

Seedlings of Peace

From the earth, tiny hopes emerge,
Whispers of faith in every surge.
Gentle winds carry peace anew,
In tender hearts, love breaks through.

Water the ground with kindness rare,
Caring hands show that we care.
In patience sown, blessings arise,
A harvest bright under endless skies.

Through stormy nights, we stand our ground,
In unity's song, a strength profound.
Roots entwined in sacred trust,
In every struggle, rise we must.

Let our voices blend as one,
A chorus sweet, a journey begun.
In diversity, harmony lies,
Together in faith, we reach for the skies.

Nurture the seedlings, let them thrive,
With love as the light, we come alive.
In every heart, let peace increase,
Together we sow the seeds of peace.

A Testament of Resilience

In storms that rage, we find our way,
With courage born of darkest day.
Hearts unbroken, spirits high,
A testament under the sky.

Rising strong from ashes bare,
Hope ignites with every prayer.
Each challenge faced, a lesson learned,
In trials deep, a fire burned.

Through shadows cast, we seek the light,
With steadfast faith, we'll win the fight.
Every setback, a step toward grace,
In love's embrace, we find our place.

Woven tales of strength untold,
In every heart, a flame of gold.
In unity we stand, aligned,
By grace and grit, our souls defined.

From struggles faced, we journey forth,
Resilience gleams, a sacred worth.
With open hearts, we'll bravely stand,
A testament of faith, hand in hand.

A Tapestry of Mercy

In shadows deep, His light breaks through,
Threads of grace in colors true.
Woven hearts, in love entwined,
A sacred promise, gently signed.

Each tear a tale, each sigh a song,
In His embrace, we all belong.
With open hands, we seek the way,
A tapestry of mercy, here to stay.

The Path to Forgiveness

On narrow roads, where burdens lie,
We cast our doubts into the sky.
With humble hearts, we bend our knee,
And find the strength to set hearts free.

The weight of sin may slow our pace,
But love will guide us through the grace.
Forgiveness blooms in tender sights,
As hope ignites our inner lights.

Renewal in Silent Prayer

In quiet moments, still and deep,
We find the peace that comforts sleep.
With whispered hopes, we seek His face,
In renewal's arms, we find our space.

Our burdens laid, our spirits soar,
Each silent prayer opens the door.
With faith anew, we rise to stand,
In His embrace, we understand.

Echoes of Redemption

From broken paths, we hear the call,
Redemption's echo, strong and tall.
In every heart, a story told,
A journey rich, with threads of gold.

Through trials faced and lessons learned,
In faith's warm glow, our hearts have burned.
With every step, we seek the light,
Echoes of love, banishing night.

Streams of Tranquility

In stillness I find my peace,
A gentle flow, my soul's release.
The waters whisper, soft and low,
In the light of grace, I glow.

Each ripple speaks of love divine,
A sacred bond, both pure and fine.
With every breath, I draw anew,
The streams of solace, deep and true.

In nature's arms, my heart shall rest,
Tempered by faith, I am blessed.
The sun ascends, a golden hue,
In tranquil streams, my spirit grew.

With every moment, I am whole,
Divine reflections touch my soul.
I drink deeply from this source,
In tranquil waters, find my course.

Let every heartbeat sing in praise,
Through life's vast journey, I will raise.
The hymn of peace, forever bright,
In streams of tranquility, pure light.

Pathways to Restoration

Through valleys low, the path unfolds,
With every step, my heart beholds.
The whispers of the ancient trails,
Guide weary souls where love prevails.

In shadows cast, the light breaks through,
A gentle hand, made just for you.
Each moment lost, now found again,
With grace and mercy, free from sin.

The journey marked with trials stark,
Yet hope ignites within the dark.
Restoration calls with every breath,
A sacred promise, life from death.

Let faith arise, let burdens cease,
In peaceful pathways, find your peace.
The road of healing stretches wide,
With every step, I walk with pride.

Through winding ways, my spirit mends,
In love's embrace, the journey bends.
Towards the dawn, I lift my gaze,
On pathways to restoration's ways.

Songs of the Redeemed

With joyful hearts, we sing as one,
A melody beneath the sun.
The notes of grace, like rivers flow,
In harmony, together grow.

Each voice a thread in woven praise,
In sacred moments, time we raise.
The songs of hope, forever ring,
In every soul, redemption's spring.

Through trials faced, our spirits soar,
In every burden, love restores.
With lifted hands, we sing aloud,
The songs of the redeemed, so proud.

In unity, our voices blend,
For every heart, a hand to lend.
The music swells, a sacred light,
Guiding souls through darkest night.

Rejoice, rejoice, for we are free,
In songs of joy, our spirits see.
Together bound, forever true,
The songs of the redeemed, in hue.

Unity in the Spirit

In every heart, a spark resides,
A flame of love that never hides.
Together we stand, hand in hand,
In unity, we make our stand.

Through trials faced, we rise once more,
A tapestry of rich rapport.
Each thread a story, woven tight,
In spirit's bond, we find our light.

With open hearts, we share the load,
On every hill, together strode.
In every smile, the warmth we feel,
Unity's grace, our common seal.

Let differences fade like morning mist,
In love's embrace, we coexist.
Together we dream, together we dare,
In unity's spirit, we find our care.

In every journey, side by side,
We walk in faith, with hearts open wide.
For in the spirit, we all unite,
In unity, our souls take flight.

Grace in Brokenness

In shattered clay, we find His mold,
The heart once heavy, now turns to gold.
Embraced by love, our fears dissolve,
In brokenness, our souls evolve.

With every tear, a lesson learned,
Through trials faced, our spirits burned.
In grace, we rise from depths of pain,
United, whole, our faith sustained.

His gentle hands, they mend our wounds,
In silence sweet, our hope attunes.
From ashes lost, a beauty grows,
In brokenness, His love bestows.

A journey shared, we walk as one,
With faith that shines like morning sun.
For in our scars, the light is cast,
In grace, our lives are free at last.

So let us sing, with voices clear,
For in our brokenness, He's near.
With every step, we find our way,
In grace we live, day after day.

A Light Unto My Path

In shadows deep, His light will guide,
Through darkest nights, He walks beside.
Each step we take, His hope ignites,
A beacon bright, through endless fights.

The whispers soft, they call my name,
In quiet storms, He stays the same.
With faith like fire, we blaze a trail,
In every doubt, His love prevails.

The road may twist; the path may bend,
Yet in His grace, I find a friend.
With every turn, I feel His hand,
In light divine, forever stand.

When burdens weigh and fears confound,
I lift my eyes; His peace I've found.
A promise kept, a truth so pure,
In faith I trust, my heart is sure.

So let the light, forever shine,
In every heart, His love divine.
With trust in Him, I'll boldly tread,
A light unto my path, He's led.

The Fellowship of Healing

In circles formed with open hearts,
The bond of love, in grace imparts.
Each story shared, a sacred thread,
In fellowship, our spirits fed.

The wounds we bear, together shared,
In silent night, we show we care.
Through laughter bright and tears that flow,
In healing grace, our faith will grow.

For every heart that's bruised and worn,
Together, we rise, in joy reborn.
With hands entwined, we face the storms,
In unity, our souls transform.

The healer's touch, so gentle, near,
In every word, we cast out fear.
With gentle prayers, we lift each soul,
In fellowship, we find our whole.

So let us gather, hearts aglow,
In love's embrace, our spirits flow.
With every step, we heal, we find,
The fellowship of hearts entwined.

The River of Forgiveness

In quiet streams where grace does flow,
The river deep, where hearts bestow.
With every drop, our burdens fade,
In forgiveness found, love is laid.

The currents strong, they wash away,
The guilt and shame that cannot stay.
In ripples soft, our souls are free,
In grace we find our unity.

The banks of hope, with mercy lined,
In every heart, a space confined.
But with each wave, we break the chains,
In rivers wide, forgiveness reigns.

A journey deep, we tread with trust,
In every heart, a dawn of rust.
Through valleys wide, our spirits soar,
In forgiveness, we're forevermore.

So let us dive, immerse, and yield,
In the river's flow, our hearts revealed.
With every splash, we take our stand,
In love and grace, forever band.

Breath of Divine Mercy

In stillness, grace descends,
Each heart, a sacred vessel.
Forgiveness whispers softly,
A balm for every soul's ache.

With open hands, we gather,
The fragments of our spirit.
Cleansing rivers flow freely,
Washing sins, uniting us.

Through trials, you are with us,
A light in darkest valleys.
In our weakness, you strengthen,
With mercy that restores life.

In every breath, your presence,
A loving breath of kindness.
We rise in hope together,
Transformed by your embrace.

In faith, we walk as one,
Bound by love, unbroken thread.
In each encounter, a promise,
Your breath, our guiding star.

Reflections in the Well of Hope

In the well, the waters shimmer,
Mirroring the light of dawn.
Each drop, a dream awakened,
Whispers of what can be.

Gathered souls by the water,
Seeker's hearts united.
In the depths, we find courage,
To rise above despair.

The ripples tell of journeys,
Winding paths through shadowed lands.
Yet hope, a constant anchor,
Draws us toward the horizon.

The sun breaks through the darkness,
Casting gold upon our fears.
In every cycle of sorrow,
A new song begins to rise.

From the well, we draw healing,
With each sip, a promise made.
Reflections of our spirit,
Shine bright in love's embrace.

The Light That Binds Us

In the stillness of the night,
A flicker in the shadows glows.
It binds our hearts together,
A tapestry of grace.

Through storms that rage and howl,
The light remains unshaken.
In every trial, it beckons,
A beacon for the lost.

With every step, we journey,
Together, hand in hand.
In love's embrace, we gather,
Strengthened in our unity.

In whispered prayers and hopes,
The light illuminates paths.
A sacred bond unbroken,
In the heart of every soul.

Let it shine through our stories,
A glow of every moment.
The light that binds us gently,
Guides us toward our purpose.

Anointing the Wounded Places

In the quiet of the morn,
Heal us where we are broken.
With tender hands, you touch,
Anointing scars with love.

In every tear that's fallen,
A sign of grace and healing.
You lift us from the ashes,
Restoring hope anew.

Through valleys deep and shadowed,
You walk beside the weary.
Anointing wounds with mercy,
Bringing peace to troubled hearts.

With every breath, we feel you,
Gentle spirit, ever near.
In the darkest of moments,
Your love, a constant guide.

As we gather in your name,
We find strength to endure.
In the echoes of your grace,
Our wounds turned into light.

Communion with the Divine

In quiet whispers, hearts do meet,
The sacred breath, a rhythm sweet.
Beneath the stars, we seek the light,
A bond of souls, both pure and bright.

Through prayer we rise, like morning dew,
In humble grace, we find what's true.
The spirit calls, a gentle guide,
In sacred love, we shall abide.

In stillness found, the world does fade,
In every heart, His light portrayed.
Together strong, our joy we share,
With every breath, we find Him there.

The Road to Calvary's Embrace

Upon the path, in shadows cast,
We walk in faith, though fraught and vast.
Each weary step, a heavy toll,
Yet towards the hope, we lift our soul.

With thorns adorned, the Savior sighs,
His love poured out, beyond the skies.
In every heart, His sacrifice,
A gift immense, in pain, suffice.

Through bitter trials, love will gleam,
In darkest nights, we hold the dream.
For every tear that falls in grief,
A glimpse of grace, our soul's relief.

A Lament for the Lost

Beneath the weight of shadows cast,
We mourn for souls, too lost, too fast.
In silent cries, the heartache flows,
Grief intertwined with love that grows.

The paths untraveled, echo deep,
In every memory, wounds we keep.
With gentle hands, we lift our prayer,
In hopes the lost may find Him there.

The echoes fade, yet love remains,
In every loss, our spirit gains.
A beacon bright, through darkest night,
In sorrow's grasp, we seek the light.

Harmonies of Healing

In sacred hymns, our voices rise,
A melody that never dies.
In brokenness, we find our peace,
Through every wound, our sorrows cease.

With every note, the heart takes flight,
In darkest times, we seek the light.
United hearts, a sacred choir,
In love's embrace, we lift Him higher.

Through trials faced, our spirits mend,
In each soft touch, God's hand extend.
The balm of grace, forever stays,
In harmonies, we find our ways.

Restoring the Spirit's Flame

In silent prayer, the soul takes flight,
Awakening dreams kissed by sacred light.
With whispers soft, the heart ignites,
Restoring hope through divine insights.

Beneath the stars, our spirits soar,
Finding solace on this hallowed floor.
The ember glows, in love's embrace,
Transforming shadows into grace.

Each tear we shed, a holy stream,
Mending the fabric of a lost dream.
In unity, we gather near,
Empowered by faith, casting out fear.

A journey marked by trials faced,
In every step, our faith is laced.
With hands uplifted, we rise as one,
Rekindling the flame, till day is done.

Let every prayer be a guiding star,
Leading us home, no matter how far.
Through every storm, we will remain,
Together we stand, restoring love's flame.

Blessed by Forgiveness

In the stillness, we find our peace,
Releasing burdens that never cease.
A gentle touch, a healing grace,
Blessed by forgiveness, we find our place.

In every heart, a story lies,
Of broken paths and whispered sighs.
But in the light, our spirits mend,
Forgiveness blooms, our truest friend.

Let go the weight of bitter past,
Embrace the love, the die is cast.
As dawn reveals the shadows flee,
We rise anew, forever free.

With open hearts, we walk this road,
Sharing grace, lightening the load.
Through kindness shared, we find our way,
In every moment, a brand-new day.

Bound by compassion, we start to heal,
Finding strength in the love we feel.
In this sacred dance, we find our song,
Blessed by forgiveness, where we belong.

The Alchemy of Love

In tender moments, our spirits blend,
Transforming hearts, where souls transcend.
With every glance, the magic flows,
The alchemy of love, in silence grows.

Through trials faced and storms we brave,
Our love a beacon, our hearts a wave.
In unity, we forge our fate,
With open arms, we celebrate.

From ashes rise, a phoenix bold,
In love's embrace, our fortune told.
With hands entwined, we break the mold,
A tapestry of warmth, unfurling gold.

In every laugh, in every tear,
A sacred bond, we hold so dear.
Within the chaos, peace we find,
The alchemy of love, divine and kind.

Let every heartbeat echo true,
In every moment, I'm lost in you.
With every breath, our spirits twine,
Creating wonders, forever enshrined.

In the Embrace of Grace

In the embrace of grace, we find our home,
Where weary souls are never alone.
With arms wide open, love's light will shine,
Guide us gently, through the divine.

In the stillness of a quiet prayer,
We gather strength, casting every care.
With faithful hearts, we walk each day,
Finding joy in forgiveness, come what may.

Through every struggle and every test,
In the embrace of grace, we find our rest.
Our spirits rise, in hope we soar,
Finding beauty on every shore.

In laughter shared and burdens light,
Together we stand, a radiant sight.
In every moment, let love embrace,
The promise of light, in the grace we chase.

With hearts aligned, we take our stand,
In the embrace of grace, hand in hand.
Through every trial, we learn to trust,
In love's sweet promise, in faith we must.

Waters of Forgiveness

In the depths, a river flows,
Cleansing hearts, where mercy glows.
Washing sins, so deep and wide,
In its stream, we will abide.

With gentle waves, the past is gone,
Renewed in faith, we carry on.
Each drop a promise, sweet and pure,
In this water, souls endure.

Gathered close, we seek the light,
In forgiveness, wrongs take flight.
Hearts once heavy, now set free,
Flowing forth, our harmony.

Let the waters guide our way,
In their embrace, we chose to stay.
Through every trial, pain and strife,
The river whispers, "Choose new life."

In the stream, we find our peace,
Where shame and doubt begin to cease.
A holy tide that lifts the soul,
In waters deep, we are made whole.

The Gift of Renewal

A dawn awakes, the sky so bright,
Each moment birthed in holy light.
From ashes rise, the spirit sings,
In every heart, the promise clings.

Renewed by grace, our burdens shed,
In quiet prayer, our spirits fed.
With every breath, we feel the change,
In love's embrace, we are estranged.

The blossoms bloom, from seeds sown deep,
In fields of faith, the harvest reap.
With open hands, we share the gift,
A soul uplifted, spirits lift.

In the cycle, life descends,
Yet in each loss, a new hope bends.
Transformation through trials we bear,
In God's design, we find His care.

Together rise, as one we stand,
In unity, we seek His hand.
The gift of renewal, ever near,
In every heartbeat, love sincere.

Nestled in Grace

In the quiet of night's embrace,
We find our peace, nestled in grace.
With whispered prayers, our spirits soar,
In this haven, we seek no more.

Each star above, a light to guide,
In faith we gather, side by side.
Through trials faced, our hearts as one,
In joy and sorrow, hope begun.

The gentle breeze that stirs the trees,
Brings whispers of love, a sacred breeze.
Upon the shores of our weary souls,
We seek the tide, as calmness rolls.

With every tear, a lesson learned,
In brokenness, the heart has turned.
Embracing grace, our burdens lift,
In divine love, we find our gift.

Together we walk, through storms and sun,
In unity, we have begun.
Nestled in grace, forever true,
In His arms, we are made new.

Penance and Peace

In shadows cast, we seek the light,
With heavy hearts, we seek what's right.
Through penance borne, our spirits mend,
In silent whispers, grace descends.

Each step we take, toward worthy ground,
In heartfelt places, love is found.
Forgiveness blooms, where mercy reigns,
In peace we gather, breaking chains.

With open hearts, our burdens shared,
In understanding, the soul is bared.
Through trials faced, we find our way,
In every tear that led to day.

Penance taught, the lesson clear,
In seeking truth, we shed the fear.
In quiet strength, we find release,
In letting go, we find our peace.

Together rise, in faith we stand,
In His embrace, we find the hand.
Penance passed, we move ahead,
In peace and love, our spirits wed.

In the Light of Divine Embrace

In shadows deep, His grace does flow,
A warmth that guides, where hearts can glow.
With open arms, He beckons near,
In every whisper, love draws near.

Through trials faced, we find our way,
In faith we walk, through night and day.
Each tear we shed, He turns to light,
In darkness cast, shines hope so bright.

O gentle hand that calms the storm,
In every doubt, He keeps us warm.
With faith renewed, our spirits rise,
In divine embrace, we see the skies.

Through sacred paths, our souls align,
In every prayer, His love we find.
With grateful hearts, we lift our song,
In light divine, we all belong.

The Well of Forgiveness

In every heart, a well of grace,
Where burdens lift and sins erase.
The waters pure, they cleanse the soul,
In humble prayer, we find the whole.

With each regret, we search for light,
Through mercy's door, we find what's right.
The past released, a new dawn shines,
In every heart, His love entwines.

Forgiveness flows like rivers wide,
In healing balm, our pains abide.
With open hearts, we let it be,
In every soul, He sets us free.

In whispered hopes, we start anew,
With love restored, our spirits true.
The well of grace, forever waits,
In forgiveness, He reinstates.

Sacred Echoes

In silence deep, the echoes call,
A gentle whisper, a heavenly thrall.
In every breath, His presence near,
In sacred moments, we hold dear.

The mountains rise, the valleys speak,
As nature's voice, we humbly seek.
In every star, a message glows,
In sacred echoes, love bestows.

Through prayer and song, our spirits soar,
In harmony, we yearn for more.
Each beating heart, a symphony,
In sacred echoes, we find unity.

The gentle breeze, the rustling trees,
In nature's breath, our souls appease.
With every wave that kisses shore,
In sacred echoes, we explore.

Mending the Frayed Edges

In weary hearts, where shadows dwell,
We seek the light, a gentle well.
With tender hands, He mends the seams,
In every tear, He plants our dreams.

Through trials faced, we find our way,
In love's embrace, our fears allay.
With faith renewed, we stand so tall,
In grace's arms, we shall not fall.

The fabric woven with threads of hope,
In every struggle, we learn to cope.
Through storms that rage, His peace remains,
In mending hearts, love breaks the chains.

For every wound, a scar divine,
In healing grace, our souls entwine.
Through frayed edges, new paths arise,
In love's embrace, we seek the skies.

Restoration in Grace

In silence we kneel, hearts laid bare,
Seeking solace, in Your care.
With every whisper, a fragile plea,
Raise our spirits, and set them free.

Through trials faced and shadows cast,
Your holy light will always last.
A gentle touch upon our soul,
In restoration, we become whole.

Through storms that rage, we find our peace,
In faith, we find our sweet release.
As grace surrounds and overflows,
Transform our hearts, as love bestows.

Oh, Shepherd kind, lead us today,
In every step, guide on our way.
With open arms, we seek Your face,
Embrace us in Your warm embrace.

With grateful hearts, we rise anew,
In the light of love, pure and true.
Together we walk, hand in hand,
Restored by grace, as You have planned.

A Prayer for the Wounded

O Lord, we bring our broken hearts,
In shadows deep, Your light imparts.
Through every wound, we seek Your balm,
Restore our souls, bring peaceful calm.

In every tear, a whispered prayer,
Hold us close, with tender care.
For all the hurt we've kept inside,
Release our fears, be our guide.

O Healer, hear this humble cry,
From depths of pain, we reach up high.
Embrace the scars that tell our tale,
In Your great love, we shall not fail.

Beneath Your wings, grant us release,
From burdens weighed, grant us peace.
In every hurt, let hope abide,
With faith unshaken, by our side.

So let us rise, renewed in light,
With every step, a sacred fight.
In love unyielding, we find our way,
For in Your arms, we will not stray.

Pilgrimage to Wholeness

Upon this path, we wander forth,
To seek our truth, to know our worth.
With every step, our spirits soar,
In search of grace, forevermore.

Through valleys low and mountains high,
We journey on, beneath the sky.
A sacred quest to find our place,
In every heartbeat, feel Your grace.

The road may twist, the night may fall,
Yet in our hearts, we heed the call.
For in the struggle, strength is found,
In every trial, we rise unbound.

O guide us on, O light divine,
In every shadow, let us shine.
With faith as fuel and love as flame,
We carry forth, in Jesus' name.

At journey's end, our spirits blend,
In wholeness true, we'll find our friend.
For in each step, we've come to know,
In unity, Your love will flow.

Tapestry of Grace

Threads of life woven with care,
In divine hands, a tapestry fair.
Each color bright, each sorrowed shade,
In Your design, all is laid.

Through joys and trials, we intertwine,
In every heart, Your love will shine.
A pattern rich, in every soul,
In unity, we become whole.

In every stitch, a story told,
Of grace unearned and love untold.
With every weave, we find our place,
In this great work, a sacred space.

O Master Weaver, guide our hands,
As we repair the broken strands.
In gentle hands, we find our way,
In every dawn, a brand new day.

So let us stand, in faith embraced,
United strong, in love encased.
For life's great loom, both vast and wide,
In You, O Lord, we shall abide.

Hands Raised in Surrender

In the quiet of the night, I bow,
Hands raised, in surrender, I vow.
Eyes closed tight, heart open wide,
In Your grace, I shall abide.

Trembling whispers escape my lips,
In this moment, my spirit dips.
Lead me through valleys of despair,
In Your love, I find my prayer.

Fears dissolve in Your embrace,
With every breath, I seek Your face.
Strength in weakness, hope to find,
In surrender, I am aligned.

In the light of dawn, I stand still,
Trusting Your plan, my heart will fill.
Every burden laid at Your feet,
In surrender, my soul's retreat.

Let the world fade, let the noise cease,
In Your presence, I find my peace.
With hands raised, I let love flow,
In surrender, I am home, I know.

Unseen Blessings

In the shadows, blessings hide,
Waiting patiently, hearts open wide.
A gentle touch, a fleeting glance,
In faith, we find our sacred dance.

Each struggle holds a hidden grace,
In trials faced, we find our place.
Miracles flow from love unseen,
In quiet moments, they intervene.

Stars align, though eyes can't see,
Faith unlocks the mystery.
With gratitude, let hearts proclaim,
Unseen blessings, in Your name.

Beneath the clouds, the sun still shines,
Whispers of hope in sacred lines.
Each heartbeat sings a song so true,
Unseen blessings, forever anew.

In the tapestry of life we weave,
Love enfolds us, we believe.
Together, we'll rise, hand in hand,
In unseen blessings, we shall stand.

The Altar of Compassion

At the altar of compassion, hearts unite,
With open arms, we share the light.
Every tear, a sacred plea,
In kindness' name, we set souls free.

Through every struggle, hands extend,
In love's embrace, we find a friend.
A gentle voice, a tender hand,
Compassion's call, let us understand.

For in the depths of earthly pain,
Sharing burdens, we break the chain.
The altar stands with grace so pure,
In love's reflection, we are sure.

Let mercy guide us on our way,
In simple acts, let kindness sway.
With every heart that we uplift,
At this altar, love becomes a gift.

Together we rise, together we fall,
In compassion's strength, we answer the call.
With hearts aligned, let us be brave,
At the altar of compassion, let love wave.

A Journey to Wholeness

On this path, I take my stride,
With faith as my compass, I abide.
Each step a whisper, each breath a prayer,
In the journey, I find You there.

Through valleys deep and mountains high,
In every shadow, Your light draws nigh.
Healing waters wash over me,
In this journey, my spirit's free.

Every wound, a story told,
In the tapestry of grace, behold.
With every trial, my soul expands,
In the journey, You hold my hands.

Hope ignites the darkest night,
In tangled paths, I seek Your light.
With every heartbeat, I find my way,
In the journey, I rise each day.

And as I walk this sacred ground,
In Your presence, my peace is found.
To wholeness, I journey, side by side,
In love's embrace, I shall abide.

Grace in the Brokenness

In the cracks where light does seep,
There lies a hope both strong and deep.
Through the pain our hearts must face,
We find His love, our saving grace.

With heavy burdens, souls may weep,
Yet in His arms, the lost are steep.
He mends the wounds, He heals the heart,
In brokenness, we're set apart.

For every tear that falls like rain,
He gathers gently, easing pain.
With every loss, a seed is sown,
In shattered lives, His mercy's shown.

In silence, whispers softly blend,
Through sorrow, He remains our friend.
A light that leads through darkest night,
In brokenness, we find His light.

So let us walk, though paths are rough,
In brokenness, we're strong enough.
For grace is found in every trial,
In humble hearts, He walks each mile.

Whispers of Redemption

In shadows deep where silence dwells,
A voice of hope, our soul compels.
Through every heartache, every tear,
Redemption calls, it draws us near.

To weary souls and spirits worn,
He comes to mend the broken thorn.
With gentle hands, He lifts the weak,
In whispered love, salvation speaks.

The past may haunt, the burden weigh,
Yet grace appears to light the way.
In every struggle, choice to strive,
His whispers keep our dreams alive.

For in the dark, we hear His song,
A melody where we belong.
In every moment, fear must flee,
Redemption wrapped in mystery.

So trust the path that winds ahead,
With whispers soft, our hearts are led.
In every trial, we rise anew,
With whispers sweet, He guides us through.

Sanctity in Sorrow

In sorrow's depth, a sacred place,
Where tears flow free, we meet His grace.
Each ache and pain a gentle call,
In our despair, He holds us all.

The heart does mourn, but also grows,
In shadows cast, the light still glows.
For in the grief, a lesson clear:
Sanctity lives when love draws near.

With every struggle, faith arrives,
In darkness deep, the spirit thrives.
Through trials faced and burdens borne,
In every loss, we are reborn.

Though heavy hearts may bend and sway,
In quietude, we find our way.
In sacred space, amidst the pain,
His love remains, forever reigns.

So let us find a blessing here,
In every tear, a story dear.
In sanctity, our hearts align,
For in our sorrow, He will shine.

Light After the Shadows

In alleys dark where shadows creep,
The dawn will break, the night shall weep.
Beneath the weight of trials fierce,
His light may shine, our doubts disperse.

With every step through endless night,
A spark ignites, revealing sight.
He guides the lost with gentle hand,
In darkness deep, our hope will stand.

Emerging from the pain we bear,
The light of faith is always there.
Each broken road, our spirits rise,
Illuminated under skies.

When shadows loom and fears abound,
His presence wraps us all around.
In whispered prayers, we find release,
In light's embrace, our souls find peace.

So journey forth, let hearts be bold,
In every tale of loss retold.
For after shadows, bright days gleam,
In faith, we find our truest dream.

Divine Interlude

In silence deep, the spirit calls,
A whisper soft where shadows fall.
With outstretched hands, we seek the light,
To find our peace in endless night.

The angels sing in harmony,
Their voices blend, a sacred key.
In every heart, a sacred spark,
Illumines paths that once were dark.

From heights of grace, the blessings flow,
A river vast, where love can grow.
In every tear, a lesson learned,
Through fires of faith, our hearts have burned.

As dawn breaks forth, our spirits rise,
With grateful hearts, we cast our sighs.
In every moment, life unfolds,
A story shared, a truth retold.

Divine embrace, we rest in you,
With every breath, we start anew.
In unity, we walk this way,
For love will guide us every day.

Seraphim's Embrace

Awash in grace, the seraph sings,
Of lofty hopes and boundless wings.
In sacred space, we find our place,
In warmth of love, we're held in grace.

Their eyes aglow, through heavens soar,
In every heart, there's music's core.
As wisdom flows, we'll never tire,
Our souls ignite with each desire.

With gentle hands, they lift our plight,
Through darkest hours, they bring the light.
In quiet days, their presence stays,
We walk in faith, love's endless ways.

The seraph's breath, a tender balm,
In every storm, it weaves a calm.
With spirits joined, we rise above,
In harmony, we share their love.

In every soul, a seraph glows,
A light of peace that ever flows.
Together bound, we'll find our wings,
In seraph's care, our spirit sings.

The Symphony of Reconciliation

In discord's clash, we find our tune,
A melody beneath the moon.
With every note, a heart entwined,
In harmony, the lost shall find.

Through trials faced, the lessons grow,
In love's embrace, we learn to flow.
Each voice to lift, each hand to lend,
In unison, we mend and blend.

The symphony, a sacred art,
Resounds in every seeking heart.
Through broken paths, we step anew,
In grace we meet, in love we grew.

In every chord, the spirits dance,
To bring together every chance.
The world may break, but still we rise,
In joyful tears, we touch the skies.

As peace descends, our hearts rejoice,
Within the song, we find our voice.
In every note, a truth laid bare,
The symphony of love we share.

In the Garden of the Spirit

In the garden where spirits bloom,
Beneath the stars, no trace of gloom.
With whispers soft, the flowers sigh,
In faith and hope, our dreams will fly.

Each petal holds a sacred prayer,
A promise breathed through fragrant air.
In gentle rains, we find the peace,
The spirit's touch will never cease.

Through winding paths, we wander free,
In nature's arms, our souls agree.
With every thought, a seed we sow,
In unity, our love will grow.

As dawn descends, the light will gleam,
In every heart, a shared dream.
Together bound, through loss and gain,
In the garden, love shall reign.

With grace bestowed, we stand in awe,
In every breath, we feel the law.
In the garden's heart, we bloom and thrive,
For in this love, our spirits strive.

The Crossroads of Sorrow

In shadows deep, the heart dost weep,
A path of pain where memories creep.
With each step taken, a choice remains,
To find the light or dwell in chains.

Whispers of hope through tears do flow,
In silence carved, the wounds bestow.
Upon this road, the faithful tread,
With love's embrace, the soul is fed.

The burden heavy, yet faith stands tall,
Amidst the echoes of a lover's call.
Guided by grace, the spirit soars,
Through the tempest, the heart restores.

Each sorrow borne shall find release,
Within the promise, a sweet peace.
For on this journey, trials refine,
To lead us closer to the divine.

At the crossroads of despair and light,
The veil is lifted, revealing sight.
In every sorrow, a lesson learned,
The flame of faith forever burned.

The Weaver's Touch

In silence strong, the weaver bends,
With thread of faith, the journey blends.
Each strand a story, woven tight,
In patterns rich, a tapestry bright.

Through trials harsh, the loom does shake,
Yet from the pain, new forms awake.
With gentle hands, the weaver guides,
Each twist and turn, the soul abides.

The colors bright, a sacred hue,
Reflecting love in every view.
With each new stitch, the heart resides,
In grace's arms, where peace abides.

In moments lost, the truth shines clear,
For every tear, a thread sincere.
In unity, the fabric grows,
A hymn of life, where spirit flows.

From darkness spun to light embraced,
The weaver's touch with love is graced.
In sacred art, our lives unrolled,
A masterpiece in faith foretold.

A Psalm of Restoration

O Lord, my heart is bowed in strife,
Restore my soul, renew my life.
In valleys low, where shadows cast,
Your guiding light, my fears surpassed.

With gentle hands, the broken mend,
In your embrace, the wounds do end.
In each lament, a sacred song,
To you, dear Father, I belong.

Above the waves, your voice I hear,
With every whisper, peace draws near.
Your mercy flows like rivers wild,
In every trial, your way beguiled.

To rise again from ashes gray,
In faith renewed, I find my way.
Your promise stands, a beacon bright,
In darkest hours, your love's my light.

With every breath, I proclaim grace,
Your guiding hand, my resting place.
In psalms of hope, my heart shall sing,
For in your name, new life you bring.

Harmonies of the Redeemed

In chorus sweet, the voices rise,
A symphony that fills the skies.
With hearts entwined, we sing as one,
In grace uplifted, love begun.

Each note a prayer, each chord a plea,
In timeless rhythms, we are free.
Against the dark, our songs resound,
In unity, our hope is found.

The melodies weave the tales we share,
Of mercy's hand and answered prayer.
From depths of woe, to heights of joy,
In every heart, His love, our buoy.

With every heartbeat, the music flows,
In sacred moments, true love grows.
As echoes linger, our spirits blend,
In harmonies that never end.

As the dawn breaks with light divine,
We sing of love that knows no line.
For in this song, our souls are healed,
In harmonies of faith revealed.

Embracing the Sacred Gifts

In the dawn's gentle light, we rise,
With hearts open wide, we seek the wise.
Nature whispers truths, divine and pure,
In every breath, our spirits endure.

Stars above, like beacons bright,
Guide our souls through the dark night.
Gratitude flows for the dawn's embrace,
In sacred gifts, we find our grace.

Life's trials, a tapestry spun,
Woven with lessons, each battle won.
From challenges faced, our strength will bloom,
In faith's embrace, we banish gloom.

With hands uplifted, we sing our song,
In community's warmth, we all belong.
The sacred pulse within us flows,
In every heart, devotion grows.

Against the storm, we stand as one,
In love and hope, our battles won.
Embracing gifts both great and small,
In sacred harmony, we heed His call.

Heartstrings of Devotion

With every heartbeat, a prayer is formed,
In the quiet moments, our souls are warmed.
Through trials faced, our spirits soar,
In devotion's dance, we're forevermore.

In the stillness, whispers of grace,
Draw us closer to the holy place.
Each step taken, a path so bright,
Guided by faith, we walk in light.

Love's tender embrace, a sacred thread,
Weaves through our lives, as journeys spread.
With each connection, a bond unfolds,
In the depths of our hearts, the truth is told.

In shadows cast, we seek the flame,
Igniting hope, we call His name.
Through every trial, our hearts entwine,
In sacred love, our souls align.

Together we rise, in praise we sing,
For every blessing, our voices ring.
Heartstrings tied in devotion's embrace,
In unity's call, we find our place.

In Quiet Reverence

In quiet moments, we bow our heads,
The whispers of silence, where Spirit spreads.
With open hearts, we seek the light,
In reverence deep, we find our might.

The sacred stillness calms our fears,
In gentle prayer, we shed our tears.
With every breath, we sense the grace,
In quietude, we find our space.

Nature sings in the rustling leaves,
A symphony of peace that never deceives.
In solitude's embrace, we connect, we grow,
The sacred voice within us flows.

From mountains high to valleys deep,
In reverent awe, His love we keep.
Through every trial, through every pain,
In quiet reverence, our hearts remain.

Each moment cherished, a sacred pause,
In the stillness, we feel the cause.
With humble hearts, we lift our eyes,
In sacred union, our spirits rise.

Hymns of New Beginnings

With dawn's first light, a new day starts,
In every soul, a hymn imparts.
With open arms, we greet the sun,
In each new beginning, our lives are spun.

The past may linger, but we release,
In present moments, we find our peace.
Through shadows cast, the light breaks through,
In songs of hope, our spirits renew.

Together we stand, a vibrant choir,
In love's embrace, we rise higher.
With voices united, we share our dreams,
In sacred moments, our purpose gleams.

Every ending leads to the start,
In faith's warm glow, we play our part.
Through trials faced, we grow and learn,
In hymns of new hope, our hearts will burn.

So let us sing with joyful hearts,
In sacred harmony, where love imparts.
For every journey is a chance to find,
The beauty of life intertwined.

A Vessel for Grace

In humble whispers, blessings flow,
Hearts open wide, letting love grow.
Each tear a journey, each smile a sign,
In sacred moments, we intertwine.

Carry the light, let it shine bright,
In darkest valleys, be the hope's light.
A gentle spirit, a forgiving heart,
From this sacred vessel, never depart.

Hands outstretched, we seek the Divine,
In every touch, His presence align.
Through trials faced, we find our grace,
A journey together, we embrace.

In quiet stillness, we hear His call,
Through storms of doubt, we will not fall.
Love is our compass, a guiding tune,
A vessel of grace, under the moon.

With every heartbeat, we sing praises high,
In the arms of faith, we shall not cry.
Through every moment, our spirits rise,
A vessel of grace, where love never dies.

The Prayerful Heartbeat

In silence profound, the heartbeats pray,
Threads of connection in night and day.
Whispers of hope, in a world so wide,
The prayerful heartbeat, our faith as a guide.

Each breath a promise, each sigh a plea,
In sacred stillness, we come to be.
Through valleys low and mountains high,
The prayerful heartbeat will never die.

With hands raised high, we yearn for peace,
In every struggle, find sweet release.
Love flows like rivers, through our veins,
A prayerful heartbeat, where joy remains.

In gatherings bright, or found in solitude,
Our prayers unite, a beautiful brood.
Through every moment, let faith impart,
The rhythm of love, the prayerful heart.

In sweet surrender, let worries cease,
With every heartbeat, embrace the peace.
From this connection, our spirits dance,
The prayerful heartbeat, our soul's romance.

Illuminated Silence

In illuminated silence, wisdom speaks,
Where every shadow, a lesson seeks.
In quiet corners, the truth unfolds,
In stillness profound, His warmth enfolds.

Each breath a prayer, each pause divine,
In moments quiet, our souls align.
The light within, ignites the night,
Illuminated silence, guiding our sight.

Fading echoes of the world so loud,
In gentle whispers, hope is avowed.
In the hush between, we find our way,
Illuminated silence will never sway.

With every heartbeat, a soft refrain,
Hearts intertwined, in joy and in pain.
Through paths unknown, we shall not fear,
In illuminated silence, He draws near.

In sacred stillness, we come alive,
Through each shared moment, our spirits thrive.
In the peace of quiet, His love persists,
Illuminated silence, where the heart exists.

Refuge in the Storm

In tempest's fury, we find our rest,
A refuge strong, where love is blessed.
When chaos rages, and doubts arise,
We seek His shelter, where comfort lies.

Hands lifted high, in prayers we stand,
Through every storm, we trust His hand.
In darkest moments, faith's light will shine,
Our refuge in the storm, His love divine.

Each wave that crashes, a chance to grow,
Through trials faced, His grace we know.
In binds of worry, we will not break,
In refuge found, our hearts awake.

With faith unyielding, we'll dance in the rain,
Through every struggle, embrace the pain.
In the eye of the storm, we'll find our way,
Refuge in the storm, brightening day.

As thunder rumbles and skies turn gray,
In faith we gather, come what may.
With hearts united, our spirits soar,
Refuge in the storm, forevermore.

Spirits Renewed

In the stillness of dawn's embrace,
Faith awakens, a gentle trace.
Hearts once heavy find their song,
In His grace, we all belong.

Broken chains, the past we leave,
With whispered hopes, we all believe.
Strengthened spirits rise anew,
In the light, our journey's true.

Gathered souls in sacred space,
United by love, we seek His face.
With every prayer, our burdens share,
In His mercy, we breathe the air.

Through trials faced, our spirit grows,
In darkened nights, His love still glows.
Together, we walk this holy road,
Trusting the gifts our Father bestowed.

As we journey on this path of light,
Let hope be our guide in the night.
With spirits renewed, we lift our voice,
In His love alone, we rejoice.

The Garden of Redemption

In the garden where flowers bloom,
Faithful hearts dispel the gloom.
Each petal kissed by morning dew,
A symbol of the love that's true.

Roots of grace entwined in earth,
In every struggle, lies rebirth.
From ashes rise, the spirit's flight,
In the garden, we find our light.

Seeds of joy planted with care,
Watered by grace, with love to share.
In every shade, His whispers call,
Within this haven, we will not fall.

Harvest time brings souls to meet,
In unity, our hearts will beat.
Gathered together for His praise,
In the garden, our voices raise.

Each blossom tells a story bright,
Of redemption born in His light.
In the garden where hope is found,
Together, we stand on holy ground.

Pillars of Light

In the shadows, His light gleams,
Pillars of faith uphold our dreams.
Guiding souls through darkest night,
In His presence, we find our sight.

Each act of love, a shining beam,
Together we weave a holy theme.
With every prayer, our spirits soar,
Pillars of light forevermore.

In unity, our hearts align,
Strength in numbers, His grace divine.
Hand in hand, we move as one,
In His promise, we are never done.

Through trials faced, we hold our ground,
In pillars of light, hope is found.
With every step, our purpose clear,
In His love, we cast out fear.

Together we rise, a shining host,
In His blessings, we find our boast.
As pillars of light, we stand so tall,
In His glory, we give our all.

The Healing Waters

By the river, peace flows free,
In the waters, we find the key.
Cleansed of burdens, hearts made whole,
With every wave, He soothes the soul.

Each drop sings of love's embrace,
In this current, we find our place.
With hands outstretched, we seek His grace,
In the healing waters, we find our pace.

As we wade through life's deep strife,
These waters reflect eternal life.
In every splash, His mercy sings,
Reviving hope that faith can bring.

When weary souls begin to tire,
In this river, we find our fire.
With each gentle flow around,
In His mercy, we are found.

So let us gather by the shore,
In the healing waters, we will store.
Cleansed and renewed, we shall depart,
With waves of love within our heart.

Guided by Celestial Love

In silence we seek the guiding light,
Heaven whispers softly in the night.
In every heart, a flame does glow,
Celestial love, our souls to grow.

Through trials faced and shadows cast,
In faith we stand, our hearts steadfast.
With every prayer, a bond we weave,
In love divine, we all believe.

The stars above, they shine so bright,
A promise given in the night.
With every step, we walk in grace,
Surrounded by love's warm embrace.

When clouds arise and doubts descend,
In love's pure light, our fears we mend.
With open hearts, we rise above,
Eternal peace, our hearts shall shove.

So let us sing of love's sweet song,
Together in faith, forever strong.
In every moment, let us seek,
Guided by love, our spirits speak.

Graceful Transformations

In dawn's embrace, a new day breaks,
With tender hope, our spirit wakes.
In love's design, we find our way,
Graceful transformations guide our stay.

Voices of angels prompt the soul,
Through trials faced, we're made whole.
In every tear, a blessing flows,
The heart transformed, a vibrant rose.

With every shadow, light must show,
In darkest nights, together we grow.
Resilience built on faith's strong ground,
In grace we rise, our purpose found.

Through the storms, we stand as one,
In light and love, our fears undone.
With open hearts, we seek the way,
In graceful transformations, we shall stay.

So let us dance in life's embrace,
With faith and love, we find our place.
From ashes rise, renewed we stand,
Embracing all as God had planned.

Hymns of the Restored

In harmony, our voices blend,
To sing of love that knows no end.
Through trials deep, our song is clear,
Hymns of the restored, we draw near.

With hands uplifted, hearts made whole,
In each refrain, healing for the soul.
The light within, it brightly shines,
A sacred trust that ever binds.

In valleys low and mountains tall,
We find our truth, through love's own call.
With every note, we rise above,
In unity, we share our love.

Through the storms that life may send,
Our faith in God will not rescind.
With joy we sing, our spirits soar,
Hymns of the restored forevermore.

So let us treasure every breath,
In love's embrace, we conquer death.
With every hymn, our hearts shall sing,
Restored in grace, our praises ring.

Threads of Hope

In tapestry of life, we weave,
Threads of hope, we shall believe.
In darkness deep, a glimmer shines,
Woven together, our hearts align.

Every struggle, a pattern neat,
In love's embrace, we find our seat.
Through pain and strife, a bond is forged,
Threads of hope, our souls engorged.

With open hands, we give, we take,
In unity, our hearts awake.
For every tear, a thread we spin,
In love's design, we find within.

When shadows loom and doubts may rise,
In faith we stand, we touch the skies.
Each thread a story, rich and vast,
Threads of hope, our futures cast.

So let us hold each other near,
In every thread, dispel the fear.
With every stitch, in love we cope,
In unity, we weave our hope.

The Radiance of Healing

In stillness, the light descends,
The whisper of grace surrounds us,
Each wound receives a tender touch,
Love's balm flows, restoring trust.

Mending hearts, the spirit sings,
As hope emerges, softly bright,
In shadows, dawn begins to rise,
Guiding souls toward the light.

The broken find their way with ease,
Embraced by warmth that overflows,
In harmony, the lost believe,
The radiance forever glows.

Each prayer is a lifted hand,
Reaching through the veils of pain,
For where faith and love entwine,
A deeper truth shall remain.

So let us walk this sacred path,
Where healing waters gently flow,
Together, in our faith we stand,
In radiance, we feel love's glow.

The Threshold of Compassion

At the door where kindness waits,
A gentle heart begins to mend,
With open arms, we bridge the space,
In shared silence, wounds can end.

Empathy's embrace does bind,
Each soul reflecting light anew,
With whispers of a kinder breeze,
Our differences fade from view.

In suffering, our spirits rise,
United through the storms we face,
We find our strength in unity,
Compassion's warm, enduring grace.

The threshold beckons every soul,
To dance in love, to softly share,
With every step, we find our guide,
In heart's deep well, we become prayer.

Together, let us cross this line,
To healing lands where mercy reigns,
In love's embrace, we shall reside,
As joy transcends all earthly pains.

Dances with Angels

In twilight's glow, the angels sway,
Their wings alight with golden grace,
They guide us through the night's embrace,
In whispered prayers, we find our way.

With every step, the path unfolds,
As cosmic music fills the air,
A symphony of love untold,
In every soul, they leave their care.

We twirl beneath the star-lit skies,
Each heartbeat echoes heaven's song,
In sacred rhythms, we arise,
With angelic hosts, we dance along.

Through trials faced and burdens borne,
The spirits lift our heavy load,
In joy, we find the light reborn,
In every prayer, an angel strode.

Together, hand in hand, we'll glide,
Through realms where light and love unite,
In dances with those from above,
Our souls ignite, embracing light.

Ascent of the Soul's Desire

In quiet moments, yearning stirs,
The soul awakens, seeks the flame,
With passion's voice, it softly purrs,
To find the path, to know its name.

Ascending heights, the spirit soars,
To realms where dreams and hope reside,
With every breath, it gently roars,
In faith and trust, we shall abide.

Each step we take, a sacred climb,
Through valleys deep and mountains high,
The heart's desire, a truth in rhyme,
In every wish, the stars reply.

Embrace the joy, release the fear,
For in our quest, we shall discern,
The light we seek is always near,
In every heart, the fire burns.

So rise, dear friend, and heed the call,
With open hearts, our souls ignite,
Together, we will conquer all,
In ascent toward the boundless light.

Whispers of Grace

In silence, hearts awaken soft,
The gentle breath of hope aloft.
A guiding light through darkest night,
Whispers of grace, pure and bright.

Faithful echoes in the still,
Awakening the trusting will.
Love flows freely, heaven's balm,
In every soul, a sacred psalm.

The weary find their strength bestowed,
As kindness lights the humble road.
In every tear, a promise made,
Together walking, unafraid.

The stars above, in peace they shine,
A promise whispered, all divine.
Each moment shared, a sacred thread,
In grace, with love, we are led.

Beyond our trials, hope remains,
Through valleys low and joyful gains.
In every heartbeat, echoes trace,
The softest touch of endless grace.

Soul's Resurgence

In shadows deep, the spirit cries,
Yet from the dark, a new dawn tries.
With every breath, the soul will rise,
A heart reborn, beneath the skies.

Through valleys bleak, the paths we tread,
With faith, our hearts and minds are fed.
In quiet prayer, the spirit stirs,
The fight within, a sacred blur.

The light of hope breaks through the pain,
A cleansing rain, a sweet refrain.
With every step, our truth revealed,
In love's embrace, our wounds are healed.

Radiant joy, in stillness found,
As heaven's grace comes all around.
From ashes rise, the soul's grand song,
In unity, we all belong.

A journey vast, with faith we climb,
In every moment, pure and divine.
Boundless life through trials unfurled,
In love's embrace, we change the world.

Through Trials of Faith

In moments fraught with heavy doubt,
A whispered prayer can lead us out.
Through trials faced, our spirits strong,
In darkest nights, we find our song.

The road is rough, yet grace will guide,
With open hearts, we won't abide.
In every test, a lesson learned,
Through fiery trials, our hearts burned.

With every tear, a strength reborn,
In shadows cast, the light is worn.
We rise again with steadfast hearts,
In unity, our hope imparts.

The mountain looms, the valleys call,
Yet faith remains, a steadfast wall.
With every step, divine embrace,
Through trials faced, we find our place.

Our spirits soar, as love ignites,
With open wings, we touch the lights.
Through trials of faith, we shall prevail,
In every moment, love's sweet tale.

Beneath the Gentle Light

In quietude, the spirit rests,
Beneath the light, our hearts are blessed.
Each whisper drifts like petals fall,
A sacred call, embracing all.

The dew of morn on sacred ground,
In every touch, love's presence found.
With grateful hearts, we rise anew,
The dawn awakens, pure and true.

When shadows linger, hope ignites,
In soft embraces, shining lights.
With every breath, we claim the day,
In gentle grace, we choose to stay.

With every step, the path unfolds,
In love's embrace, our truth upholds.
In harmony, we find our might,
Together shining, bold and bright.

Beneath the stars, our souls entwine,
In sacred rhythm, love divine.
With gentle light, we rise each day,
In faithfulness, we find our way.

The Sanctuary Within

In silence I seek the holy space,
A refuge where my soul finds grace.
Whispers of peace fill the air,
God's love echoes everywhere.

Beneath the weight of worldly strain,
I turn my heart from fear to gain.
In stillness, the spirit learns to see,
The sanctuary that dwells in me.

Each breath a prayer, each thought a light,
Illuminating paths through the night.
Within this heart, a sacred dome,
In faith, I discover my true home.

The walls are made of hope and trust,
In this hallowed ground, I must.
With every step, I find the way,
To honor grace in each new day.

Here lies a journey, pure and deep,
A treasure safe, my heart to keep.
In the sanctuary of the soul,
I am made whole, I am made whole.

Rebirth of a Believer

From ashes of doubt, a flame anew,
Cleansed in the waters, my spirit grew.
In darkness I found the light that shines,
A melody sweet, heaven's designs.

With each dawn, a promise unfolds,
A rising sun, life's story told.
In trials faced, my faith is strong,
Rebirth sings in a sacred song.

Chains of the past, now scattered dust,
In the hands of love, I place my trust.
The old is gone, a vision clear,
In the heart of the believer, no fear.

With courage borne of divine embrace,
A journey starts, framing grace.
In every step, the truth revealed,
The spirit's strength, forever sealed.

Reborn I stand, in holy light,
With open arms, I soar to flight.
In this new life, I will abide,
With faith as my guide, my heart, my pride.

Embrace of the Divine

In the stillness, I feel Your hand,
A gentle touch, a love so grand.
Wrapped in whispers, I lose my way,
Finding solace, come what may.

Through shadows cast, I seek Your face,
In every trial, a warm embrace.
You lift the burdens, calm the storm,
In Your presence, my heart is warm.

With every heartbeat, my spirit calls,
In moments fleeting, or when hope falls.
Embraced in faith, I rise to see,
The beauty of Your love in me.

From mountain high to valley low,
You guide my steps, the path I know.
In every tear, a lesson learned,
In every joy, Your love returned.

With open wings, I soar with grace,
In the embrace of the Divine, I find my place.
Eternal light, forever mine,
In sacred trust, my spirit shines.

Kindling the Sacred Flame

A flicker glows in hearts refined,
The spark of faith, forever kind.
Through trials faced, adversity braved,
The sacred flame, our spirits saved.

With every whisper, the fire grows,
In love's embrace, our essence knows.
To light the dark, to warm the cold,
A story written, ages old.

Together we gather, hands entwined,
In unity's power, hearts aligned.
The sacred flame shall never wane,
In every joy, in every pain.

When storms arise and shadows creep,
Within our hearts, the flame shall leap.
Kindled with purpose, hope ignites,
Through faith's embrace, we scale new heights.

A beacon bright for all to see,
The sacred flame, our legacy.
In every step, with love we'll strive,
Together in faith, we will survive.

Charting the Stars of Trust

In the night sky, hope shines bright,
Each star a promise, a guiding light.
With hearts aligned in love's embrace,
We find our way through time and space.

Faith's gentle whisper calms our fears,
Through every trial, our vision clears.
In shadows deep, we seek the flame,
For trust is forged in love's own name.

As we chart the stars, our spirits rise,
In unity, we break the skies.
With every step, we pave the way,
To brighter tomorrows, come what may.

Together we stand, hand in hand,
In the tapestry of faith, we understand.
Each thread woven with dreams anew,
In the heart of trust, we find what's true.

In moments of doubt, we anchor strong,
The stars remind us we belong.
With love as our compass, we will soar,
Charting the heavens, forevermore.

Awakening the Quiet Soul

In silence, the spirit stirs and wakes,
A gentle touch, the stillness breaks.
Through whispered prayers, we seek to know,
The depths of peace that softly flow.

Each breath a hymn, each thought a prayer,
In quietude, we find what's rare.
The soul's awakening, profound and pure,
In sacred spaces, we feel secure.

With every dawn, the light unfolds,
A story of faith in whispers told.
In solitude, we turn within,
The journey starts where silence begins.

Be still, and hear the heart's soft call,
In faith's embrace, we rise and fall.
In moments hush, the truth appears,
Awakening the quiet soul, it clears.

Through trials faced, the soul will grow,
In sacred trust, we learn to flow.
A dance of light, a song so sweet,
In every pause, we find our feet.

The Pillars of Strength

In times of trial, we find our base,
The pillars of strength, in love, we trace.
With hearts united, we stand so tall,
In faith's embrace, we'll never fall.

With every storm, we gather might,
Together we'll shine, our spirits bright.
For every challenge, we hold the key,
In unity, we rise, and we see.

Each pillar forged with trust and care,
Supporting one another, always there.
Through darkest nights and brightest days,
In shared resolve, we find our ways.

Let love be the foundation strong,
In the heart of grace, we all belong.
With every heartbeat, every breath,
The pillars of strength defy all death.

In trials faced, we find our ground,
The echoes of faith, a resounding sound.
With courage kindled, we will ascend,
In the arms of strength, our spirits blend.

Courage Born from Faith

In shadows cast, a spark ignites,
Courage born from faith takes flight.
With every step, the heart expands,
Walking boldly in steadfast stands.

Through storms we bear, our spirits rise,
In trust and hope, we touch the skies.
With faith as shield in battles fought,
Courage flows in every thought.

Let whispers of doubt be drowned in grace,
In the light of love, we find our place.
Each challenge met with strength anew,
In faith's embrace, we see it through.

With hearts ablaze, we journey on,
Courage whispers in the dawn.
Through every tear and every cheer,
Faith holds us close and draws us near.

So let us rise with courage bold,
In the love of faith, our dreams unfold.
Together we walk, hand in hand,
With courage born from faith, we stand.

The Blessing of Brokenness

In the shadows we wander, so lost,
Yet in cracks, His light can be found.
Every tear tells a story of grace,
In the brokenness, we feel His sound.

A heart that aches finds a gentle mend,
Amidst the struggle, His love unfolds.
He gathers the pieces, calls them whole,
In our fractures, His truth beholds.

When hope seems distant, we search for peace,
In the shattering, we learn to stand.
His hands rebuild what life has torn,
In the chaos, we take His hand.

With every trial, we rise anew,
From the ashes, a spirit soars.
His mercy flows like a river's tide,
Through brokenness, our heart restores.

Let us sing of grace from shattered dreams,
For in our wounds, we find His song.
In the blessings of brokenness, we learn,
With love, we truly belong.

Divine Embrace of Healing

In stillness, we wait for the touch so pure,
A gentle whisper guides our soul.
In the chaos, He brings us peace,
With every heartbeat, we feel His whole.

Mountains may tremble, the waters roar,
Yet in His arms, we find our place.
A divine embrace that heals our wounds,
In His presence, we seek His grace.

Every ache turned into a song,
As He wraps us in loving light.
Through valleys deep, He walks beside,
In the darkness, we find our sight.

The broken and battered, He lifts above,
Restoration flows like a flowing stream.
In the divine embrace, we come alive,
In His love, we dare to dream.

Let faith be our anchor, strong and sure,
For healing comes in the quiet night.
In the sacred folds of His tender hold,
We rise anew, transformed in light.

Miriam's Song of Renewal

With tambourine in hand, we dance,
Miriam sings of hope restored.
In the waters parted, we find our way,
Every heartbeat echoes His word.

Across the sands, we tread with grace,
In joyful rhythms, our spirits soar.
For every trial faced, we stand awake,
With faith unshaken, we seek much more.

Her voice, a beacon through the years,
A melody woven in sacred trust.
In renewal, we shed the past,
With every step, we rise from dust.

In the wilderness, where doubts may roam,
His promise guides us through the night.
Together we journey, hand in hand,
With Miriam's song, we claim our light.

So let us sing, let the heavens hear,
With hearts united, we'll raise our sound.
In the harmony of grace so near,
In renewal, His love's profound.

Gathering the Fragments

Upon the altar, we bring our pain,
Each fragment, a story of grace.
In the quiet, He gathers each piece,
Remaking our hearts in His embrace.

From shattered dreams to hopes reborn,
He gathers the remnants of our days.
In His mercy, our spirits rise,
In every struggle, He gently plays.

The scattered bits of broken hearts,
In the tapestry of love, entwined.
He weaves a masterpiece of strength,
In the fragments, true beauty we find.

As we offer our scars to the Lord,
He takes our pain and transforms our fears.
In every piece that's brought to light,
He writes redemption across the years.

Let us rejoice in the love we share,
In gathering fragments, we meet His gaze.
Through every heartache and every loss,
We stand united, singing His praise.

Sanctum of Solace

In quiet corners, mercy flows,
Beneath the shadows, love bestows.
Hearts entwined in sacred grace,
Finding peace in this holy space.

Whispers soft in the gentle night,
Guiding souls towards the light.
In every breath, a prayer is said,
In faith we rise, in doubt we're led.

The storm may rage, the tempest roar,
Yet here within, we're evermore.
A refuge made from tears and strife,
In this sanctum, we find life.

Together we weave, hopes and dreams,
In the warmth of love, our spirit beams.
Here the world fades, worries cease,
In the embrace of divine peace.

Let the soul's song echo wide,
In faith united, we shall abide.
Beyond the trials, we will soar,
In this hallowed sanctum, forevermore.

Resurgence of the Soul

From ashes rise the spirit bright,
In darkest hours, there shines the light.
A journey forged in pain and grace,
In every step, we find our place.

With every tear, a seed is sown,
In depths of sorrow, love is grown.
From shadows cast, new paths will start,
As hope ignites the weary heart.

The battles fought, the lessons learned,
In quiet strength, our passions burned.
Through trials faced, we claim our name,
In humble hearts, we seek the flame.

Echoes linger, whispers clear,
In every struggle, God is near.
The sacred spark begins to glow,
In the resurgence, we shall know.

Together we rise, hand in hand,
The promise made, forever stand.
In faith reborn, our spirits free,
In every heartbeat, eternity.

Mending Through Faith

Beneath the burdens that we bear,
A gentle touch, a answered prayer.
In shattered hopes, we find the way,
With mending hearts, we greet the day.

The scars we hold, they tell the tale,
Of journeys faced when dreams grow pale.
Yet in the stillness, grace does flow,
In faith we find the strength to grow.

Through trials deep, and doubts that bind,
In sacred moments, peace we find.
The fabric woven, threads of light,
In unity, our spirits bright.

The healing love that knows no end,
In every heart, a willing friend.
With open souls, we lift the veil,
In mending faith, we shall prevail.

So let us rise, in purpose stand,
Together strong, hand in hand.
In every heartbeat, life's embrace,
With faith, we mend; with love, we trace.

A Sacred Journey Within

In quietude, the spirit wakes,
Through silent paths, the heart it takes.
A journey deep, where shadows play,
In sacred whispers, truth shall stay.

The stars above, they shine with grace,
Guiding footsteps through time and space.
With each encounter, wisdom flows,
In every moment, love bestows.

Through valleys low and mountains high,
In sacred trust, we learn to fly.
With every breath, a sacred hymn,
Awakening the light within.

In solitude, the echoes ring,
A dance of life in everything.
Embrace the stillness, seek the dawn,
In sacred journey, we move on.

So let the spirit lead us forth,
Discovering beauty, revealing worth.
In sacred paths, our souls entwine,
In this journey, we shall shine.

A Covenant of Love

In the quiet dawn, His promise shines,
A bond unbroken, through the divine.
He whispers softly, hearts entwined,
In every tear, His grace we find.

Through trials faced, we learn to trust,
In love's embrace, we rise from dust.
With open hands, we share our plight,
Guided together, toward the light.

In every prayer, our spirits soar,
A sacred pact forevermore.
With faith and hope, we walk this way,
In harmony, we choose to stay.

The world may wane, yet love will grow,
In kindness sown, a gentle glow.
Through darkness deep, our hearts ignite,
Together forever, a guiding light.

So let us walk, this path of grace,
With every step, His warm embrace.
In love we find, our truest song,
In this covenant, we all belong.

Steps Toward the Light

In shadows deep, we seek the dawn,
With each new step, we carry on.
The path may twist, but faith will guide,
A beacon bright, our hearts abide.

Though fears may rise, we hold on tight,
Each whispered prayer, a spark of light.
With open eyes, we see so clear,
In every moment, He is near.

The road may wane, but hope prevails,
In every heartache, love reveals.
With hands held high, we face the day,
In grace we walk, and not astray.

Through trials faced, we grow more bold,
Our stories shared, in faith retold.
With every breath, we find our place,
In steps toward light, we see His grace.

Let spirits rise, to heights unknown,
In unity, we find our home.
As one, we stand, our voices strong,
In steps toward light, we all belong.

The Breath of the Afflicted

In silence deep, the weary call,
A gentle breath, to bridge us all.
With heavy hearts, we seek His peace,
In every sigh, our sorrows cease.

Through pain endured, we reach for grace,
His love abides in every place.
With trembling hands, we lift our voice,
In faith and hope, we make our choice.

The spirit weak may find its rest,
In love's embrace, we are blessed.
Through trials faced, we learn to bind,
In every struggle, strength we find.

So let us breathe, in Him we trust,
In every moment, hope is just.
Through scattered dreams, a vision clear,
In every breath, He draws us near.

With hearts awake, we seek the light,
Embracing joy, dispelling night.
In breath of love, we find our voice,
In every heart, we all rejoice.

Forgiving Shadows

In shadows cast, we find our way,
With grace and mercy, we gently sway.
Forgiveness flows like rivers wide,
In healing hearts, we turn the tide.

The past may linger, yet we must rise,
In letting go, we seek the skies.
With open hearts, we mend the seams,
In every pain, we hold our dreams.

Through trials faced, we learn to see,
The power of love, to set us free.
In whispered prayers, we make amends,
In every heart, His love transcends.

With courage deep, we face our fears,
In acts of kindness, dry our tears.
Through forgiving shadows, we find grace,
In unity, we embrace our place.

So let us walk, this path of light,
With open arms, we end the night.
In forgiving hearts, we learn to fly,
In love we soar, our spirits high.

Murmurs of Serenity

In whispers soft, the spirit sighs,
As dawn brings light to shadowed skies.
A peace that flows, a gentle stream,
In quiet moments, we find our dream.

Through trials faced, true grace will show,
In every step, we learn and grow.
With faith's embrace, our hearts align,
In sacred stillness, all is divine.

The stars above, like lanterns glow,
Guiding our paths, where love will flow.
In the silence, hear the call,
Murmurs of hope, uniting all.

Let burdens lift, let joys arise,
In unity, we touch the skies.
With every prayer, the soul's relief,
In murmurs soft, we find belief.

A tranquil heart, a hopeful muse,
In gentle faith, we shall not lose.
Through life's embrace, we find our way,
In murmurs of serenity, we pray.

Wings of Rest

Upon the winds, our spirits soar,
To heights unseen, we long for more.
With weary hearts, we seek the nest,
In arms of love, we find our rest.

Each feather soft, a silent prayer,
In every breath, the sacred air.
With faith as wings, we rise above,
In tranquil grace, we find His love.

Through storms that rage and trials deep,
In trust we walk, in light we leap.
The clouds may part, the sun will shine,
In wings of rest, the heart aligns.

Let burdens fall, like autumn leaves,
In whispered calm, the spirit believes.
With tender grace and peace bestowed,
On wings of rest, we share the road.

In every pause, a moment's peace,
In joyful hearts, our fears will cease.
With wings of rest, we rise anew,
In sacred trust, our spirits flew.

Faithful Rebirth

From ashes rise, the soul renewed,
In love's embrace, our hearts pursued.
In shadows cast, the light breaks through,
A faithful rebirth, the spirit's view.

With every tear, a lesson learned,
In trials faced, our hearts have turned.
Through winter's chill, the spring will greet,
In faithful rebirth, we find our feet.

The past may fade, yet wisdom stays,
In humble paths, we learn to praise.
With hands outstretched, we seek the light,
In faithful rebirth, our souls take flight.

Let hope revive, as seasons change,
In every heartbeat, life feels strange.
With courage born from depths we face,
In faithful rebirth, we find our place.

In prayers whispered, a journey starts,
In every ending, new dreams are parts.
With faithful rebirth, we rise above,
Awakened now, in light and love.

A Heart Made Whole

In gentle grace, the heart unfolds,
With every story softly told.
Through trials faced and lessons learned,
A heart made whole, where love has turned.

With every ache, a strength we find,
In faith's embrace, we leave behind.
The broken pieces, once in pain,
In unity, our hearts remain.

Through love's sweet song, we mend the seams,
In laughter shared, we weave our dreams.
The cracks of life, they tell our tale,
In harmony, we shall not fail.

With hands entwined, we journey on,
In every dusk, a hopeful dawn.
Through every tear, we rise and sing,
A heart made whole, a sacred offering.

With every beat, a promise stays,
In restless nights, our spirits blaze.
Together we stand, and thus we know,
A heart made whole will always glow.

Chasing Heavenly Rainbows

In the sky where colors dance,
We look above, and take a chance.
With faith our guide, we'll rise so high,
Chasing dreams that never die.

Through trials faced, our spirits soar,
With every drop, we seek for more.
Beneath the light, we find our way,
In sacred hues, we pause to pray.

The storms may come, but hope remains,
In every tear, love breaks the chains.
Embracing grace, we'll walk the path,
In the light of joy, we find our worth.

With every glimpse of paradise,
We know His heart, we pay the price.
For in His arms, the lost are found,
In rainbow hues, His love abounds.

As we pursue, our spirits bright,
In faith, we chase eternal light.
Each step of faith, a bright embrace,
In heavenly rainbows, we find grace.

Clothe Me in Kindness

Wrap me in garments soft and warm,
Let charity be my guiding charm.
With every act, my heart I share,
In gentle hands, love's burden bear.

Let kindness flow like rivers wide,
In every place, my heart abide.
In humble moments, let me see,
The grace in you, the grace in me.

In whispers sweet and actions pure,
Through every trial, love shall endure.
So clothe my soul in mercy's thread,
In every word and prayer I spread.

Oh grant me strength to lift the weak,
The silent cry, the broken speak.
In kindness sown, may seeds take flight,
Through every heart, let there be light.

In every gaze, let kindness bloom,
Transform the world, dispel the gloom.
As garments worn, love's grace shall shine,
In acts of kindness, hearts entwine.

Beneath the Wings of Mercy

In shadows deep, where troubles lie,
I seek your grace, my spirit nigh.
Beneath Your wings, I find my peace,
In every storm, my fears release.

Your gentle touch, it calms my soul,
In Your embrace, I am made whole.
With whispered love, You fill the air,
With every breath, I feel your care.

Through trials faced, my heart will soar,
With every cry, You hear me more.
Beneath the wings that shelter me,
In Your embrace, my heart is free.

So let me dwell in mercy's light,
Each step I take, guided by might.
In every prayer, a refuge found,
Beneath the wings where love abounds.

May I extend this mercy wide,
Embracing all who seek to hide.
With open arms, let me be true,
Beneath Your wings, I walk with You.

Rock of Ages

In times of trial, I find my stand,
On You, O Lord, my solid land.
Through waves that crash and winds that blow,
You are my strength, my heart's true flow.

When shadows fall and darkness calls,
Your light remains, it never stalls.
The faithful promise, ever near,
In every heartache, quells my fear.

Oh Rock of Ages, strong and true,
In every challenge, see me through.
With steadfast love, You hold the key,
To everlasting victory.

In times of joy and pain alike,
I turn to You, my Savior's light.
With open heart, I seek Your face,
In every season, find Your grace.

So let my life be built on You,
In every word and action, too.
The Rock of Ages shall remain,
Through every storm, through every pain.

Heart of Flesh

Transform my heart from stone to grace,
In tenderness, let love embrace.
With every beat, let kindness grow,
In depths of mercy, let me sow.

Oh, heart of flesh, so pure and true,
Reflect the love, I find in You.
In gentle whispers, guide my way,
In every moment, let me stay.

With every pulse, Your love ignites,
In every struggle, shine Your lights.
As rivers flow, let grace abound,
In every heartbeat, peace be found.

So teach me, Lord, to love anew,
To see the world with eyes so true.
In every face, Your image shines,
In heart of flesh, true love aligns.

Embrace the weary, lift the weak,
In loving words, let mercy speak.
Oh, heart of flesh, forever bound,
In every heartbeat, love resounds.